KNOWLEDGE
AT YOUR FINGERTIPS

KNOWLEDGE
AT YOUR FINGERTIPS

Dr. Jose B. Caringal

To order additional copies of this book, contact:
Xlibris Corporation
1-888-795-4274
www.Xlibris.com
Orders@Xlibris.com
36593

DEDICATED

TO THOSE WHO KNOW BUT WHO FORGET

*AND MOST OF ALL TO MY WIFE GRACE, MY SON
CONRAD AND MY DAUGHTER MIA*

PREFACE

This book is unique in itself because of the absence of a Table of Contents. It would be similar to that of a dictionary but by no means a complete and thorough digest or in no way will replace a textbook. The contents may stimulate the reader to do more knowledge acquisition and research. The subjects are arranged in alphabetical order and therefore will facilitate the search of a topic. Paradoxically, day to day topics and uncommon subjects are intermingly printed in this book. They are arranged as much as possible in an outline form and in the utmost simplicity for easy reading and recall. Supplements and improvements are always in progress. The table of contents may be in the offing if the book enlarges.

I hope, as the title of the book implies, the reader will have an easy access to the subject matter. Ex. Mythology will fall under the letter M. Also Money will be under M but of course will precede Mythology. Constant use and acquaintance with the book will enable the reader to locate the topics with ease.

The main sources of my information are from my personal experience and background, several textbooks, various dictionaries and encyclopedias.

The writing of this book was made possible thru the help of my wife, Grace and my two children, Conrad and Mia whose criticism compelled me to do more researches and alterations.

At the last part of the book, there are some "Fun Words" to learn and play. Ample space is provided on each page to add more of your own information and input. Also suggestions and corrections are most welcome. You may wish to send copies to me for the next edition. Please state your source of information. This would be much appreciated. Reasonable mailing expenses will be refunded to you if published in the next edition. Your name will also be placed in the next printing as a contributor. Thank you.

DR. JOSE B. CARINGAL
13449 PERIWINKLE AVE
SEMINOLE, FL 33776

ALPHABETS
****

1.	A	ALPHA	A α		
2.	B	BETA	B β		
3.	C	CH, KH, CHI	X χ		
4.	D	DELTA	Δ δ		
5.	E	EPSILON	E ε		
6.	F	PH, PHI	Φ φ		
7.	G	GAMMA	Γ γ		
8.	H	ETA	H η		
9.	I	IOTA	I ι		
10.	J				
11.	K	KAPPA	K κ		
12.	L	LAMBDA	Λ λ		
13.	M	MU	M μ		
14.	N	NU	N ν		
15.	O	OMICRON	O o	OMEGA	Ω ω
16.	P	Pi	Π π	Ps, Psi	Ψ ψ
17.	Q				
18.	R	RHO	P ρ		
19.	S	SIGMA	ε, σ, S		
20.	T	TAU	T τ	TH THETA	Θ θ
21.	U				
22.	V				
23.	W				
24.	X	XI	Ξ ξ		
25.	Y	UPSILON	Υ υ		
26.	Z	ZETA	Z ζ		

AMERICAN CONSTITUTION
****

PREAMBLE

We the People of the United States, in Order to form a more perfect Union, establish Justice, insure domestic Tranquility, provide for the common defence, promote the general Welfare, and secure the Blessings of Liberty to ourselves and our Posterity, do ordain and establish this Constitution for the United States of America.

There are 7 articles and 26 amendments.

ARTICLE
- I------- LEGISLATIVE POWERS
- II------ EXECUTIVE POWERS
- III----- JUDICIAL POWERS
- IV----- POWERS OF THE STATE
- V------ THE CONGRESS
- VI----- SUPREME LAW OF THE CONSTITUTION
- VII---- RATIFICATION OF THE CONVENTIONS OF NINESTATESANDTHEINDEPENDENCE OF THE UNITED STATES

AMENDMENTS
- I------- FREEDOM OF RELIGION, SPEECH AND PRESS
- II------ THE RIGHT TO KEEP AND BEAR ARMS
- III----- RIGHTS OF THE SOLDIER
- IV----- RIGHTS OF PRIVACY AND DOMICILE
- V------ RIGHTS OF AN INDIVIDUAL DUE PROCESS OF LAW AND COMPENSATION
- VI----- FAIR TRIAL OF AN ACCUSED
- VII---- RIGHT OF TRIAL BY THE JURY
- VIII--- NO EXCESSIVE FINES OR PUNISHMENT
- IX----- HUMAN RIGHTS BEYOND THE BILL OF RIGHTS
- X------ RIGHTS OF EACH STATES

AMERICAN STATES	FLOWERS	BIRDS
****************************	***************	**********

UNITED STATES ....GOLDEN ROD ....BALD EAGLE

	AMERICAN STATES	FLOWERS	BIRDS
1	ALABAMA (AL)	CAMELIA	YELLOW HAMMER
2	ALASKA (AS)	FORGET-ME-NOT	ALASKA WILLOW
3	ARIZONA (AR)	CACTUS BLOSSOM	CACTUS WREN
4	ARKANSAS (AK)	APPLE BLOSSOM	MOCKINGBIRD
5	CALIFORNIA (CA)	GOLDEN POPPY	QUAIL
6	COLORADO (CO)	COLOMBINE	LARK BUNTING
7	CONNECTICUT (CT)	MOUNTAIN LAUREL ...	ROBIN
8	DELAWARE (DE)	PEACH BLOSSOM	BLUE HEN
9	FLORIDA (FL)	ORANGE BLOSSOM ...	MOCKINGBIRD
10	GEORGIA (GA)	CHEROKEE ROSE	BROWN THRASHER
11	HAWAII (HI)	RED HIBISCUS	HAWAIIAN GOOSE
12	IDAHO (ID)	SYRINGA	BLUE BIRD
13	ILLINOIS (IL)	VIOLET	CARDINAL
14	INDIANA (IN)	PEONY	CARDINAL
15	IOWA (IO)	WILD ROSE	GOLD FINCH
16	KANSAS (KA)	SUNFLOWER	MEADOW LARK
17	KENTUCKY (KY)	GOLDEN ROD	CARDINAL
18	LOUISIANA (LA)	MAGNOLIA	BROWN PELICAN
19	MAINE (ME)	PINE CONE	CHICKADEE
20	MARYLAND (MD)	BLACK-EYE SUSAN	ORIOLE
21	MASSACHUSETTS (MA) ...	MAYFLOWER	CHICKADEE
22	MICHIGAN (MI)	APPLE BLOSSOM	ROBIN
23	MINNESOTA (MN)	LADY'S SLIPPER	LOON
24	MISSISSIPPI (MS)	MAGNOLIA	MOCKINGBIRD
25	MISSOURI (MO)	HAWTHORN	BLUEBIRD
26	MONTANA (MT)	BITTERROOT	MEADOW LARK
27	NEBRASKA (NE)	GOLDEN ROD	MEADOW LARK
28	NEVADA (NV)	SAGEBRUSH	BLUEBIRD
29	NEW HAMPSHIRE (NH)	LILAC	PURPLE FINCH
30	NEW JERSEY (NJ)	VIOLET	GOLDFINCH
31	NEW MEXICO (NM)	YUCCA FLOWER	ROADRUNNER
32	NEW YORK (NY)	ROSE	BLUEBIRD
33	NORTH CAROLINA (NC) ...	DOGWOOD	CARDINAL

34 NORTH DAKOTA (ND) ...PRAIRIE ROSE ....MEADOW LARK
35 OHIO (OH) ....CARNATION ....CARDINAL
36 OKLAHOMA (OK) ....MISTLETOE ....SCISSOR-TAILED
                                                               FLYCATCHER
37 OREGON (OR) ....OREGON ....GRAPE MEADOW
                                                               LARK
38 PENNSYLVANIA (PA) ......MOUNTAIN LAUREL RUFFED GROUSE
39 RHODE ISLAND (RI) ......VIOLET ....RHODE ISLAND
                                                               RED
40 SOUTH CAROLINA (SC) ....YELLOW JESSAMINE ...WREN
41 SOUTH DAKOTA (SD) ......PASQUE FLOWER ......RINGED-NECKED
                                                               PHEASANT
42 TENNESSEE (TN) ....IRIS ....MOCKINGBIRD
43 TEXAS (TX) ....BLUEBONNET ....MOCKINGBIRD
44 UTAH (UT) ....SEGO LILY ....SEA GULL
45 VERMONT (VT) ....RED CLOVER ....HERMIT THRUSH
46 VIRGINIA (VA) ....DOGWOOD ....CARDINAL
47 WASHINGTON (WA) ......RHODODENDRON ...GOLDFINCH
48 WEST VIRGINIA (WV) ....RHODODENDRON ...CARDINAL
49 WISCONSIN (WI) ....VIOLET ....ROBIN
50 WYOMING (WY) ....INDIAN PAINT...........BRUSH MEADOW
                                                               LARK

AMERICAN GOVERNMENT AND FLAG
****

LEGISLATIVE

1) Senate—2 senators from each State
2) House of Representative—435 members with resident commissioner of Puerto Rico who has the right to speak and to make motions but not to vote.

EXECUTIVE
1) President
2) Vice-president

JUDICIAL
1) 1 chief and
2) 8 associates of the Supreme Court

SUCCESSION TO THE OFFICE OF THE PRESIDENCY

PRESIDENT
VICE-PRESIDENT
SPEAKER OF THE HOUSE
SECRETARY OF THE STATE

FLAG
****

7—red stripes
6—white stripes
50—stars

PLEDGE OF ALLEGIANCE
"I pledge allegiance to the flag of the United States of America and to the Republic for which it stands, one Nation under God indivisible, with liberty and justice for all."

AMERICAN STATES AND CAPITALS
****

UNITED STATES .... WASHINGTON D.C.

1	ALABAMA (AL)	MONTGOMERY
2	ALASKA (AS)	JUNEAU
3	ARIZONA (AR)	PHOENIX
4	ARKANSAS (AK)	LITTLE ROCK
5	CALIFORNIA (CA)	SACRAMENTO
6	COLORADO (CO)	DENVER
7	CONNECTICUT (CT)	HARTFORD
8	DELAWARE (DE)	DOVER
9	FLORIDA (FL)	TALLAHASSEE
10	GEORGIA (GA)	ATLANTA
11	HAWAII (HI)	HONOLULU
12	IDAHO (ID)	BOISE
13	ILLINOIS (IL)	SPRINGFIELD
14	INDIANA (IN)	INDIANAPOLIS
15	IOWA (IO)	DES MOINES
16	KANSAS (KA)	TOPEKA
17	KENTUCKY (KY)	FRANKFORT
18	LOUISIANA (LA)	BATON ROUGE
19	MAINE (ME)	AUGUSTA
20	MARYLAND (MD)	ANNAPOLIS
21	MASSACHUSETTS (MA)	BOSTON
22	MICHIGAN (MI)	LANSING
23	MINNESOTA (MN)	ST. PAUL
24	MISSISSIPPI (MS)	JACKSON
25	MISSOURI (MO)	JEFFERSON CITY
26	MONTANA (MT)	HELENA
27	NEBRASKA (NE)	LINCOLN
28	NEVADA (NV)	CARSON CITY
29	NEW HAMPSHIRE (NH)	CONCORD
30	NEW JERSEY (NJ)	TRENTON
31	NEW MEXICO (NM)	SANTA FE
32	NEW YORK (NY)	ALBANY
33	NORTH CAROLINA (NC)	RALEIGH

34 NORTH DAKOTA (ND) .... BISMARK
35 OHIO (OH) .... COLUMBUS
36 OKLAHOMA (OK) .... OKLAHOMA CITY
37 OREGON (OR) .... SALEM
38 PENNSYLVANIA (PA) .... HARRISBURG
39 RHODE ISLAND (RI) .... PROVIDENCE
40 SOUTH CAROLINA (SC) .... COLUMBIA
41 SOUTH DAKOTA (SD) .... PIERRE
42 TENNESSEE (TN) .... NASHVILLE
43 TEXAS (TX) .... AUSTIN
44 UTAH (UT) .... SALT LAKE CITY
45 VERMONT (VT) .... MONTPELIER
46 VIRGINIA (VA) .... RICHMOND
47 WASHINGTON (WA) .... OLYMPIA
48 WEST VIRGINIA (WV) .... CHARLESTON
49 WISCONSIN (WI) .... MADISON
50 WYOMING (WY) .... CHEYENNE

AMERICAN STATES AND MOTTOS
****

UNITED STATES	NICKNAMES

1	ALABAMA (AL)	THE COTTON STATE
2	ALASKA (AS)	THE LAST FRONTIER
3	ARIZONA (AR)	THE GRAND CANYON STATE
4	ARKANSAS (AK)	THE WONDER STATE
5	CALIFORNIA (CA)	THE GOLDEN STATE
6	COLORADO (CO)	THE CENTENNIAL STATE
7	CONNECTICUT (CT)	THE CONSTITUTION STATE
8	DELAWARE (DE)	THE DIAMOND STATE
9	FLORIDA (FL)	THE SUNSHINE STATE
10	GEORGIA (GA)	THE EMPIRE STATE OF THE SOUTH
11	HAWAII (HI)	THE ALOHA STATE
12	IDAHO (ID)	THE GEM STATE
13	ILLINOIS (IL)	THE LAND OF LINCOLN
14	INDIANA (IN)	THE HOOSIER STATE
15	IOWA (IO)	THE HAWKEYE STATE
16	KANSAS (KA)	THE SUNFLOWER STATE
17	KENTUCKY (KY)	THE BLUEGRASS STATE
18	LOUISIANA (LA)	THE PELICAN STATE
19	MAINE (ME)	THE PINE TREE STATE
20	MARYLAND (MD)	THE OLD LINE STATE
21	MASSACHUSETTS (MA)	THE BAY STATE
22	MICHIGAN (MI)	THE WOLVERINE STATE
23	MINNESOTA (MN)	THE GOPHER STATE
24	MISSISSIPPI (MS)	THE MAGNOLIA STATE
25	MISSOURI (MO)	THE SHOW ME STATE
26	MONTANA (MT)	THE TREASURE STATE
27	NEBRASKA (NE)	THE CORNHUSKER STATE
28	NEVADA (NV)	THE SAGEBRUSH STATE
29	NEW HAMPSHIRE (NH)	THE GRANITE STATE
30	NEW JERSEY (NJ)	THE GARDEN STATE
31	NEW MEXICO (NM)	THE LAND OF ENCHANTMENT
32	NEW YORK (NY)	THE EMPIRE STATE

33 NORTH CAROLINA (NC) .... THE TAR HEEL STATE
34 NORTH DAKOTA (ND) ..... THE FLICKERTAIL STATE
35 OHIO (OH) .... THE BUCKEYE STATE
36 OKLAHOMA (OK) .... THE SOONER STATE
37 OREGON (OR) .... THE BEAVER STATE
38 PENNSYLVANIA (PA) .... THE KEYSTONE STATE
39 RHODE ISLAND (RI) .... THE LITTLE RHODY STATE
40 SOUTH CAROLINA (SC) ... THE PALMETTO STATE
41 SOUTH DAKOTA (SD) .... THE SUNSHINE STATE
42 TENNESSEE (TN) .... THE VOLUNTEER STATE
43 TEXAS (TX) .... THE LONE STAR STATE
44 UTAH (UT) .... THE BEEHIVE STATE
45 VERMONT (VT) .... THE GREEN MOUNTAIN STATE
46 VIRGINIA (VA) .... THE OLD DOMINION
47 WASHINGTON (WA) .... THE EVERGREEN STATE
48 WEST VIRGINIA (WV) .... THE MOUNTAIN STATE
49 WISCONSIN (WI) .... THE BADGER STATE
50 WYOMING (WY) .... THE EQUALITY STATE

PRESIDENTS OF THE UNITED STATES
****

		TERM	BORN	DIED	AGE
1	GEORGE WASHINGTON (F) ...	1789-1797 --	1732 --	1799 --	67
2	JOHN ADAMS (F)	1797-1801 --	1735 --	1826 --	91
3	THOMAS JEFFERSON (D-R)	1801-1809 --	1743 --	1826 --	83
4	JAMES MADISON (D-R)	1809-1817 --	1751 --	1836 --	85
5	JAMES MOORE (D-R)	1817-1825 --	1758 --	1831 --	73
6	JOHN QUICY ADAMS (D-R) ...	1825-1829 --	1767 --	1848 --	81
7	ANDREW JACKSON (D)	1829-1837 --	1767 --	1845 --	78
8	MARTIN VAN BUREN (D)	1837-1841 --	1782 --	1862 --	80
9	WILLIAM HARRISON (W)	1841-1841 --	1773 --	1841 --	68
10	JOHN TYLER (W)	1841-1845 --	1790 --	1862 --	72
11	JAMES POLK (D)	1845-1849 --	1795 --	1849 --	54
12	ZACHARY TAYLOR (W)	1849-1850 --	1784 --	1850 --	66
13	MILLARD FILMORE (W)	1850-1853 --	1800 --	1874 --	74
14	FRANKLIN PIERCE (D)	1853-1857 --	1804 --	1869 --	65
15	JAMES BUCHANAN (D)	1857-1861 --	1791 --	1868 --	77
16	ABRAHAM LINCOLN (R)	1861-1865 --	1809 --	1865 --	56
17	ANDREW JOHNSON (R)	1865-1869 --	1808 --	1875 --	67
18	ULYSSES S. GRANT (R)	1869-1877 --	1822 --	1885 --	63
19	RUTHERFORD HAYES (R)	1877-1881 --	1822 --	1893 --	71
20	JAMES GARFIELD (R)	1881-1881 --	1831 --	1881 --	50
21	CHESTER ARTHUR (R)	1881-1885 --	1830 --	1886 --	56
22	GROVER CLEVELAND (D)	1885-1889 --	1837 --	1908 --	71
23	BENJAMIN HARRISON (R)	1889-1893 --	1833 --	1901 --	68
24	GROVER CLEVELAND (D)	1893-1897 --	1837 --	1908 --	71
25	WILLIAM MCKINLEY (R)	1897-1901 --	1843 --	1901 --	58
26	THEODORE ROOSEVELT (R) ...	1901-1909 --	1858 --	1919 --	61
27	WILLIAM TAFT (R)	1909-1913 --	1857 --	1930 --	73
28	WOODROW WILSON (D)	1913-1921 --	1856 --	1924 --	68
29	WARREN HARDING (R)	1921-1923 --	1865 --	1923 --	58
30	CALVIN COOLIDGE (R)	1923-1929 --	1872 --	1933 --	61
31	HERBERT HOOVER (R)	1929-1933 --	1874 --	1964 --	90
32	FRANKLIN ROOSEVELT (D)	1933-1945 --	1882 --	1945 --	63

33 HARRY TRUMAN (D) .... 1945-1953 -- 1884 -- 1972 -- 88
34 DWIGHT EISENHOWER (R) .... 1953-1961 -- 1890 -- 1969 -- 79
35 JOHN F. KENNEDY (D) .... 1961-1963 -- 1917 -- 1963 -- 46
36 LYNDON JOHNSON (D) .... 1963-1969 -- 1908 -- 1973 -- 65
37 RICHARD NIXON (R) .... 1969-1974 -- 1913 -- 1994 -- 81
38 GERALD FORD (R) .... 1974-1977 -- 1913 -- 2006 -- 93
39 JAMES CARTER (D) .... 1977-1981 -- 1924
40 RONALD REAGAN (R) .... 1981-1989 -- 1911
41 GEORGE BUSH (R) .... 1989-1993 -- 1924
42 WILLIAM CLINTON (D) .... 1993-2001 -- 1946
43 GEORGE WALKER BUSH 2001   -- 1946

ANIMALS (GROUP-HERD)
****

ANTS	COLONY
ASSES	PACE
BEARS	SLEUTH
BEES	HIVE, SWARM
BIRDS	FLIGHT
CATTLE	DROVE
CATS	CLOWDER, CLUSTER, CLUTTER, LITTER
CHICKS	BROOD, CLUTCH
CROWS	MURDER
CLAMS OR OYSTERS	BED
DOGS	LITTER
DUCKS	BRACE
EAGLES	CONVOCATION
ELKS	GANG
ELEPHANTS	HERD
FISH	DRAUGHT, SCHOOL, SHOAL
FOXES	SKULK
FROGS	ARMY
GOATS	TRIBE, TRIP
GEESE	GAGGLE, SKEIN
GORILLAS	JAYS, BAND
GNATS	HORDE, CLOUD
HARES	HUSK, DOWN
HORSES	PAIR, TEAM
HAWKS	CAST
KITTENS	KINDLE
LARKS	EXALTATION
LEOPARDS	LEAP
LIONS	PRIDE
MULES	BARREN
MONKEYS	TRIBE
PEACOCKS	MUSTER
PHEASANTS	NEST, NYE, NIDE
PIGS	LITTER
QUAIL	BEVY

SHEEP .... FLOCK
SEALS .... POD, SIGNET
STORKS .... MUSTERING
SPARROWS .... HOST
SQUIRREL .... DRAY
TROUT .... HOVER
TURTLES .... BALE
VIPER .... NEST
WHALES .... GAM
WOLVES .... PACK

ANIMALS
****

	YOUNG	MALE	FEMALE
ASS	FINNY, FOAL		
BEAR	CUB		
BIRD	NESTLING		
CAT	KITTEN		
CHICKEN	CHICK, PULLET	ROOSTER, COCK	HEN
COW	CALF	BULL	COW
DEER	FAWN	STAG, HART	DOE
DOG	PUP	DAM	BITCH
DONKEY	JENNET		
DUCK	DUCKLING		
EAGLE	EAGLET		
ELEPHANT	CALF		
FISH	FRY, FINGERLING		
FOX	CUB		
FROG	TADPOLE		
GOAT	KID		
GOOSE	GOSLING	GANDER	
HAWK	EYAS		
HORSE	COLT, FILLY, FOAL	STALLION, SIRE	MARE
INSECT	PUPA		
KANGAROO	JOEY		
LION	CUB	LION	LIONESS
MONKEY	BABY		
MOOSE	CALF		
OTTER	WHELP		
OYSTER	SPAT		
PIG	PIGLET, SHOAT, FARROW	BOAR	SOW
RABBIT	BUNNY		
RHINOCEROS	CALF		
SALMON	PARR		
SEAL	PUP		

SHARK	TOPE		
SHEEP	LAMB, TEG	RAM	EWE
SWAN	CYGNET	COB	PEN
TIGER	CUB		TIGRESS
TURKEY	POULT		
WHALE	CALF		
WOLF	CUB		
ZEBRA	COLT		

ANNIVERSARIES
****

1ST	-	PAPER
2ND	-	COTON
3RD	-	LEATHER
4TH	-	FLOWERS, FRUIT
5TH	-	WOOD
6TH	-	CANDY, SUGAR, IRON
7TH	-	COPPER, WOOL
8TH	-	POTTERY, BRONZE
9TH	-	POTTERY, WILLOW
10TH	-	TIN, ALUMINUM
11TH	-	STEEL
12TH	-	LINEN, SILK
13TH	-	LACE
14TH	-	IVORY
15TH	-	CRYSTAL
20TH	-	CHINA
25TH	-	SILVER
30TH	-	PEARL
35TH	-	CORAL
40TH	-	RUBY
45TH	-	SAPPHIRE
50TH	-	GOLD
55TH	-	EMERALD
75TH	-	DIAMOND

BIRTHSTONES AND FLOWERS
****

JAN	GARNET	CARNATION
FEB	AMETHYST	VIOLET
MAR	AQUAMARINE	JONQUIL
APR	DIAMOND	SWEET PEA
MAY	EMERALD	LILY OF THE VALLEY
JUN	PEARL	ROSE
JUL	RUBY	LARKSPUR
AUG	PERIDOT	GLADIOLUS
SEPT	SAPPHIRE	ASTER
OCT	OPAL	CALENDULA
NOV	TOPAZ	CHRYSANTHEMUM
DEC	TURQUOISE	NARCISSUS

ZODIAC SIGNS
****

JAN 20	--	FEB 18	--	AQUARIUS
FEB 19	--	MAR 20	--	PISCES
MAR 21	--	APR 19	--	ARIES
APR 20	--	MAY 20	--	TAURUS
MAY 21	--	JUN 20	--	GEMINI
JUN 21	--	JUL 22	--	CANCER
JUL 23	--	AUG 22	--	LEO
AUG 23	--	SEP 22	--	VIRGO
SEP 23	--	OCT 21	--	LIBRA
OCT 22	--	NOV 21	--	SCORPIO
NOV 22	--	DEC 21	--	SAGITTARIUS
DEC 22	--	JAN 19	--	CAPRICORN

(♒) WATER BEARER
(♓) FISHES
(♈) RAM
(♉) BULL
(♊) TWINS
(♋) CRAB
(♌) LION
(♍) VIRGIN
(♎) SCALE OR BALANCE
(♏) SCORPION
(   ) ARCHER
(   ) GOAT

BIOLOGY—STUDY OF LIVING THINGS
****

CLASSIFICATIONS OF ANIMALS AND PLANTS IN DESCENDING ORDER

1)   KINGDOM
2)   PHYLUM
3)   CLASS
4)   ORDER
5)   FAMILY
6)   SPECIES

COLORS
****

PRIMARY	SECONDARY

RED   RED + BLUE = = = = PURPLE
BLUE   BLUE + YELLOW = GREEN
YELLOW   YELLOW + RED = = ORANGE

PRISM—POLYHEDRON TWO SIDES AS BASES

LIGHT ------------   ----------------RED
                               --------------ORANGE
                               ------------YELLOW
                               ---------- GREEN
                               -------- BLUE
                               ------- VIOLET

RAINBOW COLORS................. RED   ....OUTER ARC
               .... ORANGE
               .... YELLOW
               .... GREEN
               .... BLUE
               .... VIOLET............INNER ARC

COMPUTER
****

I.   COMPUTER PARTS:

      CPU -   CENTRAL PROCESSING UNIT
               IBM & COMPATIBLES
                    PC ----- PERSONAL COMPUTER
                    PCjr---- PERSONAL COMPUTER (SMALLER)
                    PS/2---- PERSONAL SYSTEM
                    XT------ EXTENDED TECHNOLOGY (w/HARD DISK)
                    AT------ ADVANCED TECHNOLOGY

      KEYBOARD
      MONITOR -   B & W— COLOR
                    MDA--- MONOCHROME DISPLAY ADAPTOR
                    CGA---- COLOR GRAPHICS ADAPTOR
                    EGA---- ENHANCED GRAPHICS ADAPTOR
                    VGA---- VIDEO GRAPHICS ARRAY
                    MCGA– MULTIPLE COLOR GRAPHICS ARRAY

II.   DOS—DISK OPERATING SYSTEM
      ASCII - AMERICAN STANDARD CODE FOR INFORMATION
                  INTERCHANGE
      RAM - RANDOM ACCESS MEMORY (ERASABLE)
      ROM - READ ONLY MEMORY (PERMANENT)

III. DISK—SINGLE & DOUBLE SIDED & DENSITY
      40 TRACKS -- ONE SIDE
      80 TRACKS -- TWO SIDES
      9 SECTORS -- ONE SIDE

      9 X 40 = 360 SECTORS
              X 2
             —

          720 TOTAL SECTORS

1 SECTOR = 512 BYTES
1 BYTE = 8 BITS = 184,320 BYTES ON ONE SIDE
1 KILOBYTE - 1,000 BYTES
1 MEGABYTE - 1,000,000 BYTES

CYLINDERS - SECTORS IN HARD DISK

SYSTEM DISK - 1. HIDDEN COMMAND (COMMAND.COM)
   BOOTABLE (IBM BIOS)
       (IBM DOS)
      2. CONFIG.SYS
      3. AUTOEXE.BAT
DATA DISK—NO HIDDEN FILES—ONLY FOR STORAGE

IV. TO FORMAT A:/V/S
  V = VOLUME (NO HIDDEN FILES)
  S = SWITCH (WITH HIDDEN FILES)

V. TO COPY
  DISKCOPY—DISK TO DISK ONLY DISKCOPY A:B: OR A: B:
  COPY A:*.* B: (IF DOES NOT WORK TRY TO PUT
  COPY TO HARD DRIVE C: SPACE BETWEEN COMMANDS!)
    MD FILENAME
    CD FILENAME
    COPY A:*.* OR COPY A:*.*C:
    BACK TO FLOPPY
    CD\FILENAME
    C:\FILENAME COPY *.*A:

VI. EXECUTABLE COMMANDS

  .COM DO NOT NEED TO EXECUTE
  .EXE CAN ONLY WORK WITH PATH COMMAND
  .BAS
  .BAT

VII. PRINTERS
    LPT1, LPT2—PARALLEL PORT CONNECTIONS
    COM1, COM2—SERIAL PORT CONNECTION
    TO PRINT—E.G. C:\DIR>PRN OR ^P—WILL PRINT DIR.
        REPEAT ^P WILL GO BACK C:\.

VIII. COMMANDS
    SWITCH ON—COLD BOOT—COMPLETE SYSTEM CHECK & CPU
    CTRL-ALT-DEL—WARM BOOT SKIPS SYSTEM CHECK
    DIR—COMPLETE WITH TIME
    DIR/W—WIDE IN ONE SCREEN
    DIR/P—PAUSES
    VER—VERIFY VERSION
    CHKDSK—CHECK DISK
    CURRENT DRIVE—SAME AS DEFAULT DRIVE
    CLS—CLEAR SCREEN
    CTRL-BREAK—STOP & BACK TO DOS
    MD—MAKE DIRECTORY
        A:\NEWS>MD TODAY
        A:\NEWS\TODAY TODAY BECOMES SUBDIRECTORY
    RD—REMOVE OR ERASE DIRECTORY
        A:\RD NEWS NEW
    ERASE OR DELETE
        CD\FILENAME
        DEL FILENAME.EXT
    PRINT—DIR>PRN
    PROMPT—TO GO BACK TO DOS; WITH $ CHANGE COMMAND
    CD:\—BACK TO THE ROOT DIRECTORY
    C>—TO REMOVE VOL.—TYPE VOL A OR LABEL A:
    CTRL S—STOPS SCREEN ROLL

IX. DEFINITIONS
    BASIC—MOST POPULAR AND PRIMARY LANGUAGE FOR
        PERSONAL COMPUTER.
    BAUD—NUMBER OF BITS THAT ARE TRANSMITTED PER
        SECOND.
    BUG—A PROBLEM IN A PROGRAM THAT PREVENTS IT FROM
        EXECUTING PROPERLY.

DEBUG—PROCESS OF FINDING AND CORRECTING ERRORS IN A PROGRAM

PIXEL—NUMBER OF DOTS IN A SPACE.

STRING VARIABLES—VARIABLES THAT CONTAIN LETTERS OR SYMBOLS RATHER THAN JUST NUMBERS. IDENTIFIED BY THE DOLLAR ($) SIGN.

SYNTAX—AN ERROR IN PROGRAMMING PROCEDURES SUCH AS A MISSPELLED WORD OR INVALID COMMAND.

COBOL—(COMMON BUSINESS ORIENTED LANGUAGE) MOST WIDELY USED LANGUAGE FOR BUSINESS APPLICATIONS. ITS MATH FUNCTIONS ARE LIMITED TO SIMPLE ARITHMETIC.

FORTRAN—(FORMULA TRANSLATION) THE MOST WIDELY USED LANGUAGE ON LARGER COMPUTERS FOR SCIENTIFIC AND ENGINEERING PROGRAMS.

LOGO—A GRAPHICS LANGUAGE, OFTEN USED TO TEACH YOUNG CHILDREN PROGRAMMING.

PASCAL—A STRUCTURED LANGUAGE THAT IS BECOMING MORE AND MORE POPULAR ON MICROCOMPUTERS.

X. TO MAKE DOC.FILE—C:\COPY CON A: WRITE FILE NAME AND ENTER, THEN WRITE DOC. & FINISH WITH A ^Z AND ENTER. THIS WILL COPY IN DISK A. DISADVANTAGE CAN NOT CORRECT. THEN USE THE EDLIN.

XI. TROUBLE SHOOTING
1. CHECK CURRENT DRIVE OR DEFAULT.
2. CHECK DISK IF WRITE PROTECT OR NOT.
3. CHECK IF DISK IS FORMATTED. ONE WAY TO FIND OUT TYPE A: CHKDSK

IX. UPDATE
ADDRESS .... TO PLACE AN E-MAIL ADDRESS
BROWSER .... NAVIGATION OF WWW OR INTERNET
BLOG .... ONLINE PERSONAL JOURNAL
DOMAIN .... AN EXTENSION AS .COM AS FOR BUSINESS, .EDU—EDUCATIONAL, .GOV—GOVERNMENT, .ORG—ORGANIZATION, .MIL—MILITARY AND .NET—NETWORK

E-MAIL................. ELECTRONIC MESSAGE
FLAME................. INAPPROPRIATE MESSAGE
FTP...................... FILE TRANSFER PROTOCOL
HTML.................. HYPERTEXT MARKUP LANGUAGE—COMPATIBLE
                     WITH WWW
INTERNET.......... GLOBAL NETWORK TO SEND E-MAIL
HTTP.................. HYPERTEXT TRANSFER PROTOCOL PRECEDES
                     WWW
MODEM.............. ALLOWS COMPUTER TO COMMUNICATE OVER
                     TELEPHONE
ROUTER.............. ALLOWS TO SEND AND RECEIVE INFORMATION
                     BETWEEN NETWORKS
URL..................... UNIFORM RESONANCE LOCATOR—AN
                     ELECTRONIC ADDRESS TO GIVE COMPLETE
                     ADDRESS AS *http://www*
SPAM................... UNNECESSARY AND UNSOLICITED E-MAIL
WWW .... WORLD WIDE WEB—INTERCONNECTED
                     INTERNET SITES

COUNTRIES AND CAPITALS
****

AFGHANISTAN .... KABUL
ALBANIA .... TIRANA
ALGERIA .... ALGIERS
ANGOLA .... LUANDA
ARGENTINA .... BUENOS AIRES
AUSTRALIA .... CANBERRA
AUSTRIA .... VIENNA
BAHAMAS .... NASSAU
BANGLADESH .... DACCA
BARBADOS .... BRIDGETOWN
BELGIUM .... BRUSSELS
BOLIVIA .... LA PAZ
BRAZIL .... BRASILIA
BULGARIA .... SOFIA
BURMA .... RANGOON
CAMBODIA .... PHNOM PENH
CANADA .... OTTAWA
CHILE .... SANTIAGO
CHINA .... BEJING
COLOMBIA .... BOGOTA
CONGO .... BRAZZAVILLE
COSTA RICA .... SAN JOSE
CUBA .... HAVANA
CYPRUS .... NICOSIA
CZECHOSLAVAKIA .... PRAGUE
DENMARK .... COPENHAGEN
DOMINICAN REPUBLIC ..... SANTO DOMINGO
EQUADOR .... QUITO
EGYPT .... CAIRO
EL SALVADOR .... SAN SALVADOR
ETHOPIA .... ADDIS ABABA
FIJI .... SUVA
FINLAND .... HELSINKI
FRANCE .... PARIS
EAST GERMANY .... BERLIN

WEST GERMANY .... BONN
GHANA .... ACCRA
GREECE .... ATHENS
GRENADA .... ST. GEORGE'S
GUATEMALA .... GUATEMALA CITY
GUINEA .... CONAKRY
GUYANA .... GEORGETOWN
HAITI .... PORT-AU-PRINCE
HAWAII .... HONOLULU
HONDURAS .... TEGUCIGALPA
HUNGARY .... BUDAPEST
ICELAND .... REYKJAVIK
INDIA .... NEW DELHI
INDONESIA .... JAKARTA
IRAN .... TEHERAN
IRAQ .... BAGDAD
IRELAND .... DUBLIN
ISRAEL .... JERUSALEM
ITALY .... ROME
JAMAICA .... KINGSTON
JAPAN .... TOKYO
JORDAN .... AMMAN
KENYA................................. NAIROBI
NORTH KOREA .... PYONYANG
SOUTH KOREA .... SEOUL
KUWAIT .... KUWAIT
LAOS .... VIENTIANE
LEBANON .... BEIRUT
LIBYA .... TRIPOLI
LUXEMBOURG .... LUXEMBOURG
MADAGASCAR .... ANTANANARIVO
MALAYSIA .... KUALA LAMPUR
MALTA .... VALLETTA
MEXICO .... MEXICO CITY
MONGOLIA .... ULAN BATOR
MOROCCO .... RABAT
MOZAMBIQUE .... MAPUTO
NEPAL .... KATHMANDU
NETHERLANDS .... AMSTERDAM

NEW ZEALAND	WELLINGTON
NICARAGUA	MANAGUA
NIGERIA	LAGOS
NORWAY	OSLO
PAKISTAN	ISLAMABAD
PANAMA	PANAMA CITY
PAPUA NEW GUINEA	PORT MORESBY
PARAGUAY	ASUNCION
PERU	LIMA
PHILIPPINES	QUEZON CITY – MANILA
POLAND	WARSAW
PORTUGAL	LISBON
RUMANIA	BUCHAREST
RUSSIA	MOSCOW
SAUDI ARABIA	RIYADH
SINGAPORE	SINGAPORE
SOLOMON ISLANDS	HONIARA
SOUTH AFRICA	PRETORIA & CAPE TOWN
SPAIN	MADRID
SRI LANKA	COLOMBO
SUDAN	KHARTOUM
SWEDEN	STOCKHOLM
SWITZERLAND	BERN
SYRIA	DAMASCUS
THAILAND	BANGKOK
TUNISIA	TUNIS
TURKEY	ANKARA
UGANDA	KAMPALA
UNITED ARAB	ABU DHABI
UNITED KINGDOM (ENGLAND)	LONDON
UNITED STATES	WASHINGTON D.C.
URUGUAY	MONTEVIDEO
VENEZUELA	CARACAS
VIETNAM	HANOI
YUGOSLAVIA	BELGRADE
ZAIRE	KINSHASA

DEFINITIONS
****

ASS .... SAME AS DONKEY
JENNY .... FEMALE DONKEY
MULE .... CROSS BETWEEN MALE DONKEY AND FEMALE
                                  HORSE (USUALLY STERILE
BURRO .... SMALL DONKEY
STREAM .... FLOWING BODY OF WATER
BROOK .... A SMALL STREAM OR RIVULET
RIVER .... A LARGE NATURAL STREAM OF WATER
STRAIT .... A NARROW PASSAGE OF WATER CONNECTING
                                  LARGE BODIES OF WATER
CANAL .... ARTIFICIAL WATERWAY
LAKE .... A LARGE BODY OF WATER ENCLOSED BY LAND
SWAMP .... MARSHY GROUND
GULF .... ARM OF SEA
OCEAN .... LARGE BODY OF SALT WATER COVERING MUCH
                                  OF EARTH
SEA .... SMALLER THAN AN OCEAN
HILL .... A HIGH PIECE OF LAND
MOUNTAIN .... A LOFTY NATURAL ELEVATION ON EARTH
                                  SURFACE
VALLEY .... LAND AREA BETWEEN HILL OR MOUNTAIN (DALE)
PLATEAU .... FLAT LAND SURFACE WITH SLOPING SIDE (MESA)
ISLAND .... BODY OF LAND SURROUNDED BY WATER
PENINSULA .... A PIECE OF LAND NEARLY SURROUNDED BY
                                  WATER
LATITUDE .... LINES RUNNING ALONG THE EQUATOR
LONGITUDE .... LINES RUNNING FROM NORTH TO SOUTH
CONTINENT .... MAJOR LAND MASS
NATION (COUNTRY) .... PEOPLE LIVING IN ONE TERRITORY UNDER SAME
                                  GOVERNMENT
GOVERNMENT .... POLITICAL GOVERNING BODY
TOWN .... SMALL CITY BUT LARGER THAN A VILLAGE
VILLAGE .... A GROUP OF HOUSES FORMING A SMALL
                                  COMMUNITY
CITY .... LARGE TOWN; MAJOR METROPOLITAN
PROVINCE .... ADMINISTRATIVE UNIT OF COUNTRY
ARCHIPELAGO .... BODY OF WATER WITH MANY ISLANDS

CAPITAL .... CITY IN WHICH THE GOVERNMENT IS LOCATED
PERENNIAL .... PERPETUAL; EVERLASTING
ANNUAL .... YEAR TO YEAR
BIANNUAL .... TWICE A YEAR; SEMIANNUAL
TORT .... A WRONGFUL CIVIL ACT
CRIME .... A BREAKING OF A LAW
MURDER .... PREMEDITATED KILLING OF A PERSON
MANSLAUGHTER .... KILLING WITHOUT PREMEDITATION OR MALICE
HOMICIDE .... KILLING OF ANOTHER PERSON
FELONY .... A GRAVE OR SERIOUS CRIME EX. MURDER OR
RAPE
MISDEMEANOR .... A LESSER CRIME EX. PARKING VIOLATION OR
PETTY THEFT
PERJURY .... INTENTIONAL GIVING OF FALSE STATEMENT
UNDER OATH
LIBEL .... DEFAMATION BY WRITTEN WORD OR WORDS
SLANDER .... DEFAMATION BY SPOKEN WORD OR WORDS
LARCENY .... ROBBERY—(PETTY—BELOW LEGAL AMOUNT)
(GRAND—ABOVE LEGAL AMOUNT)
BIGOTRY .... PREJUDICE OR INTOLERANCE OF A BELIEF OR
OPINION
ACT .... A FUNCTION
ADMINISTRATION .... MANAGEMENT
ORGANIZATION .... GROUP TO PUT TO ORDER
AGENCY .... ORGANIZATION MAINLY TO OFFER AID
INSTITUTION .... ORGANIZATION, SOCIETY, FOUNDATION OR
ESTABLISHMENT FOR PUBLIC EDUCATION OR
CHARITY
ASSOCIATION .... ORGANIZATION FOR A COMMON PURPOSE OR
STRUCTURE
CORPORATION .... AN ASSOCIATION OF PEOPLE UNDER THE
AUTHORITY OF LAW EXISTING INDEPENDENT OF
ITS MEMBERS
INCORPORATION .... THE ACT OF FORMING A LEGAL CORPORATION
ACADEMY .... A SCHOOL OR COLLEGE, AN ASSOCIATION OR
ESTABLISHMENT HAVING A SPECIFIC SUBJECT
FOR TRAINING
COLLEGE .... AN INSTITUTION OF HIGHER LEARNING
UNIVERSITY .... AN INSTITUTION OF THE HIGHEST LEARNING WITH
COLLEGES OF SPECIALIZED GRADUATE STUDIES
SCHOOL .... A COLLEGE OR UNIVERSITY TO TEACH ANY
SUBJECT

DEFINITIONS
****

ANTHOLOGY ....COLLECTION OF WRITINGS

ANTHROPOLOGY ....STUDY OF MANKIND

ASTROLOGY ....STUDY OF THE STARS IN RELATION OF HUMAN BEHAVIOUR

BIOLOGY ....STUDY OF LIVING MATTER

BOTANY............................STUDY OF PLANT LIFE

CHRONOLOGY ....ORDER OF OCCURRENCE OF PAST EVENTS

GEOGRAPHY ....STUDY OF THE EARTH'S SURFACE AND CLIMATE

GEOLOGY ....STUDY OF THE PHYSICAL STRUCTURE OF THE UNIVERSE

GEMOLOGY......................STUDY OF THE NATURAL AND ARTIFICIAL GEMSTONES

HOROLOGY......................MAKING OF TIMEPIECES AND MEASUREMENT OF TIME

OTOLOGY ....STUDY OF THE EAR AND HEARING

PHILATELY ....STUDY AND COLLECTION OF STAMPS

PHILOLOGY......................STUDY OF LITERARY TEXTS AND HISTORICAL LINGUISTICS

PHILOSOPHY....................STUDY OF TRUTH AND KNOWLEDGE

PHRENOLOGY ....THEORY OF MENTAL PROCESSES IN RELATION TO THE SHAPE OF THE SKULL

PHYSIOLOGY....................STUDY OF THE FUNCTIONS OF LIVIMG ORGANISMS

PSYCHIATRY ....STUDY OF MENTAL DISORDERS AND TREATMENT

THEOLOGY ....STUDY OF GOD

THEOREM.........................RULE EXPRESSED IN EQUATION AND FORMULA

THEORY ....EXPLANATION OF A CONJECTURAL COHERENT PRINCIPLE

TRILOGY ....A SERIES OF THREE

ZOOLOGY.........................STUDY OF ANIMAL LIFE

NOTES

EXPONENTS
****

$10^1 = 10$	KILO—10^3	MILLI—10^{-3}
$10^{-1} = .1 = 1/10$	MEGA—10^6	MICRO—10^{-6}
$10^3 = 1000 = 1 \times 10^3$	GIGA—10^9	NANO—10^{-9}
$10^{-3} = .001 = 1/1000$	MICROMICRO or	PICO—10^{-12}
$2000 = 2 \times 10^3$	MICRO—SMALL	MACRO—BIG

FRACTION (RATIO)
****

1 = 1/1= WHOLE NUMBER
1/2 = .50 = 50%
1/3 = .333 = 33%
1/4 = .25 = 25%
1/5 = .20 = 20%
1/6 = .166 = 16.6%

NUMERATOR
_____ = QUOTIENT
DENOMINATOR

PROPER FRACTION ....QUOTIENT LESS THAN 1 EX. 2/5
IMPROPER FRACTION ...QUOTIENT MORE THAN 1 EX. 5/2
SIMPLE FRACTION.........NUMERATOR AND DENOMINATOR ARE
                              WHOLE NUMBER
COMPLEX FRACTION ...NUMERATOR OR DENOMINATOR OR
                              BOTH COULD BE FRACTION OR MIXED
                              FRACTION
MIXED FRACTION ....A WHOLE NUMBER AND FRACTION
LCD ....LEAST COMMON DENOMINATOR

FRACTIONS
****

$1/2 + 3/5$ or $5/10 + 6/10$ or $\dfrac{5+6}{10} = \dfrac{11}{10} = 1\ 1/10$ ans.

$6\ 1/3 - 2\ 3/4 = 6\ 4/12 - 2\ 9/12\ (5+12/12 + 4/12) - 2\ 9/12 =$
$(5\ 16/12) - 2\ 9/12 = 3\ 7/12$ ans.

$2\ 1/3 = 3x2+1 = 7/3 = 2\ 1/3$ ans.

$2\ x\ 1/3 = \dfrac{2\ x\ 1\ 2}{3} = \dfrac{2}{3}$ ans.

$\dfrac{2}{12}\ x\ \dfrac{4}{6}\ x\ \dfrac{10}{12} = \dfrac{1\ x\ 2\ x\ 5}{6\ x\ 3\ x\ 6} = \dfrac{10}{108} = \dfrac{5}{54}$ ans.

$\dfrac{2}{3}\ ./.\ 4 = \dfrac{2}{3}\ ./.\ \dfrac{4}{1} = \dfrac{2}{3}\ x\ \dfrac{1}{4} = \dfrac{2}{12} = \dfrac{1}{6}$ ans.

$4\ ./.\ \dfrac{2}{3} = \dfrac{4}{1}\ ./.\ \dfrac{2}{3} = \dfrac{4}{1}\ x\ \dfrac{3}{2} = \dfrac{12}{2} = 6$ ans.

GEOGRAPHY
****

CONTINENTS

ASIA
AFRICA
NORTH AMERICA
SOUTH AMERICA
ANTARTICA
EUROPE
AUSTRALIA

OCEANS

ATLANTIC
ARCTIC
INDIAN
PACIFIC

MAJOR DESERTS

SAHARA ....N. AFRICA
GOBI ....MONGOLIA, CHINA
MOJAVI ....S. CALIFORNIA
PAINTED DESERT ....N. ARIZONA

GEOLOGY
****

ARCHEOZOIC)   (FIRST SIGN OF LIFE)
                ------------------ 3,000,000,000 YEARS)
PROTEROZOIC)

PALEOZOIC
    CAMBRIAN .... (FIRST MARINE ....50,000,000 YRS)
    ORDOVICIAN .... (FIRST FISH ....70,000,000 YRS)
    SILURIAN .... (LAND LIFE ....20,000,000 YRS)
    DEVONIAN .... (AMPHIBIANS ....50,000,000 YRS)
    CARBONIFEROUS ... (REPTILES, SHARKS ....75,000,000 YRS)
    PERMIAN .... (INSECTS ....45,000,000 YRS)

MESOZOIC
    TRIASSIC .... (DINASOURS ....45,000,000 YRS)
    JURASSIC .... (BIRDS ....45,000,000 YRS)
    CRETACEOUS .... (MAMMALS, PLANTS .....75,000,000 YRS)

CENOZOIC
    TERTIARY .... (MODERN MAMMALS ...65,000,000 YRS)
    QUARTERNARY ...... (MAN ....1,000,000 YRS)

GRAMMAR
****

TENSES

ONE OF THE THINGS <u>IS</u>   <u>SOME</u> OF YOU <u>ARE</u>

10 % OF THE APPLES <u>ARE</u>   <u>MANY</u> OF YOU <u>ARE</u>

10% OF THE APPLE <u>IS</u>   <u>THE</u> LUGGAGE <u>IS</u>

THE HEN AND CHICKEN <u>ARE</u>   <u>PIECES</u> OF LUGGAGE <u>ARE</u>

THE HEN WITH THE CHICKEN <u>IS</u>   THIS <u>IS</u>—THESE <u>ARE</u>

A FEW SCATTERED PIECES OF PAPER IS

TO WHOM IT MAY CONCERN

TO WHOM IT MAY BE ADDRESSED

THERE IS FISH IN THE MARKET

THERE ARE FISHES IN THE OCEAN (SPECIES)

ARTICLE .... PART OF A SENTENCE OR SPEECH TO
                INDICATE A NOUN
                        EX. DEFINITE...........THE
                                INDEFINITE.......A OR AN
NOUN .... THE SUBJECT OF A SENTENCE OR SPEECH
PRONOUN .... PART OF SPEECH THAT SUBSTITUTES FOR A
                NOUN
VERB .... A WORD THAT DESCRIBES AN ACTION OR
                STATE
ADJECTIVE .... PART OF SPEECH TO DESCRIBE OR MODIFY A
                NOUN
ADVERB .... PART OF SPEECH TO DESCRIBE AN ADJECTIVE

GRAMMAR
****

WHO—PERSONAL
WHICH—IMPERSONAL

(TO) WHOM SHALL I GIVE THIS BOOK?
THE GIRL WHO(M) HE SPOKE TO. (EITHER ONE)
THIS IS (I, HE, SHE)
SHE IS OLDER THAN I
HE PREFERS HER THAN (ME, HER, HIM)

HAS <u>ANYONE</u> SEEN THE BOOK?

CAN <u>ANY ONE</u> OF YOU SWIM? (DENOTES A MEMBER OF A GROUP AND
FOLLOWED USUALLY BY "OF")

INVENTIONS
****

AIRPLANE	ORVILLE & WILBUR WRIGHT—U.S. (1903)
AUTOMOBILE	KARL BENZ—GERMANY—(1885)
BAROMETER	TORRICELLI—ITALY—(1643)
BICYCLE	KARL VON SAUERBRONN—GER.—(1816-18)
CATHODE RAY TUBE	CROOKES—ENGLAND—(1878)
CLOCK	I HSING & LIANG LING-TSAN—CHINA—(725)
COMPASS	ARABS (800)
COMPUTER	VANNEVAR BUSH—U.S. (1930)
COMPUTER CHIPS	NOYCE & KIRBY
DIESEL ENGINE	RUDOLF DIESEL—GERMANY—(1892)
DYNAMITE	NOBEL—SWEDEN (1867)
ELECTROCARDIOGRAPH	HANS BERGER—GERMANY (1903)
ELEVATOR	OTIS—U.S.—(1852)
FLUSH TOILET	JOSEPH BRAHMAL—ENGLAND—(1778)
GEIGER COUNTER	GEIGER—GERMANY (1908)
GUN POWDER	CHINESE—CHINA (800)
GYROSCOPE	BOHNNEUBERGER—GERMANY—(1908)
HELICOPTER	SIKORSKY—U.S. (1939)
LASER	GORDON GOULD—U.S.—(1957)
LEVER	ARCHIMEDES—GREECE—(200 B.C.)
LIGHTNING ROD	BENJAMIN FRANKLIN—U.S. (1752)
LOCOMOTIVE	TREVITHICK—WALES—(1804)
MACHINE GUN	GATLING—U.S.—(1862)
MICROSCOPE	HANS & JANSSEN—NETHERLANDS (1590)
MICROWAVE OVEN	PERCY L. SPENCER—U.S.—(1945)
MOTION PICTURE	CAMERA THOMAS A. EDISON—U.S. (1891)
PARACHUTE	GARNERIN—FRANCE—(1797)
PEN BALL POINT	JOHN LOUD—U.S. (1888)

PIANO .... GROUP INVENTION
POLAROID LAND CAMERA .... EDWIN LAND—U.S.—(1947)
RADAR .... ALBERT TAYLOR & LEO YOUNG—
                                        U.S.—(1922)
RADIO..................................... MARCONI—ITALY—(1895)
REVOLVER .... SAMUEL COLT—U.S.—(1835)
SEWING MACHINE .... THIMONNIER—FRANCE—(1841)
                                        ELIAS HOWES—U.S.—(1846)
STETHOSCOPE .... LAENNEC—FRANCE—(1819 ?)
TELEGRAPH........................... SAMUEL MORSE—U.S.—(1832-37)
TELEPHONE.......................... ALEXANDER GRAHAM BELL—U.S.—
                                        (1875-76)
TELESCOPE........................... LIPPERSHEY—NETHERLANDS—
                                        (1608)
TELEVISION .... VLADMIR K. ZWORYKIN—U.S.—
                                        (1869)
TYPEWRITER........................ CHRISTOPHER L. SHOLES)
.... CARLOS GLIDDEN) U.S. (1867)
VACUUM CLEANER .... MCGAFFEY—U.S.—(1869)
VELCRO................................. G E O R G E   D E   M E S T R A L—
                                        SWITZERLAND—(1948)
VIOLIN................................... GROUP INVENTION
WASHING MACHINE........... HAMILTON SMITH—U.S.—(1858)
WATCH .... PETER HENLEIN—GERMANY—
                                        (1500)
WHEEL................................... SUMERIANS—(3300 B.C.)
X-RAY.................................... W I L H E L M   R O E N T G E N—
                                        GERMANY—(1895)
ZIPPER .... WHITCOMB JUDSON—U.S.—(1891)

LANGUAGES
****

ACHTUNG	ATTENTION; RESPECT
ADIEU	GOODBYE
AD INFINITUM	FOREVER
AD HOC	IMPROVISED OR IMPROMPTU REACTION FOR SPECIAL CASE
AD LIB	SPONTANEOUS OR EXTEMPORANEOUS
ALA CARTE	ACCORDING TO THE MENU
ALOHA	GREETING
BONA FIDE	GENUINE OR SINCERE
CAFE AU LAIT	COFFEE WITH CREAM
COUP D'ETAT	STROKE OF THE STATE
C'EST LA VIE	THAT'S LIFE
CHAISE	LOUNGE LOUNGING CHAIR
GESUNHEIT	HEALTH
HOR'S D'OEUVRE	SMALL PIECES OF APPETIZING FOOD
MAGNA CUM LAUDE	HIGH PRAISE
SHALOM	PEACE
SINE QUA	NON IMPORTANT; INDISPENSABLE
SUMMA CUM LAUDE	HIGHEST PRAISE
SAVOIR FAIRE	ABILITY
TETE A TETE	HEAD TO HEAD; FACE TO FACE
TOUR DE FORCE	TRICK OF FORCE
NOM DE PLUME	PEN NAME
EXEMPLI GRATIA	FOR EXAMPLE (e.g.)
ID EST	THAT IS (i.e.)
ENGLISH	I LOVE YOU
SPANISH	YO TE AMO
FRENCH	JE VOUS AIME
GERMAN	ICH LIEBE DICH
ITALIAN	TI AMO
JAPANESE	AI SHITE IMASU
RUSSIAN	YA LUBLU VAS
GREEK	S'AGAPO
PHILIPPINES (TAGALOG)	INI-IBIG KITA
POLAND	JA CIE KACHAM

MATHEMATICS
****

ADDITION   123)—ADDEND
     + 345)—ADDEND
       ―――――
       468 —SUM

SUBTRACTION   22—MINUEND
     - 11—SUBTREHEND
       ―――――
      11—DIFFERENCE

MULTIPLICATION   22—MULTIPLICANT
      x   2—MULTIPLIER
       ―――――
      44—PRODUCT

DIVISION 44 (DIVIDEND)

$$\frac{44\ (DIVIDEND)}{2\ (DIVISOR)} = 22\ (QUOTIENT)$$

QUADRILATERAL—ANY FOUR SIDED PLANE FIGURE

PARALLELOGRAM—FOUR SIDED PLANE FIGURE
    OPPOSITE SIDES ARE PARALLEL AND EQUAL

—RECTANGLE—A PARALLELOGRAM ALL ANGLES
ARE RIGHT ANGLES

—SQUARE—A PARALLELOGRAM FOUR EQUAL
SIDES AND FOUR RIGHT ANGLES

*NOTE: A RECTANGLE IS NOT A SQUARE BUT A SQUARE IS A RECTANGLE BUT BOTH ARE PARALLELOGRAMS AND QUADRILATERALS.

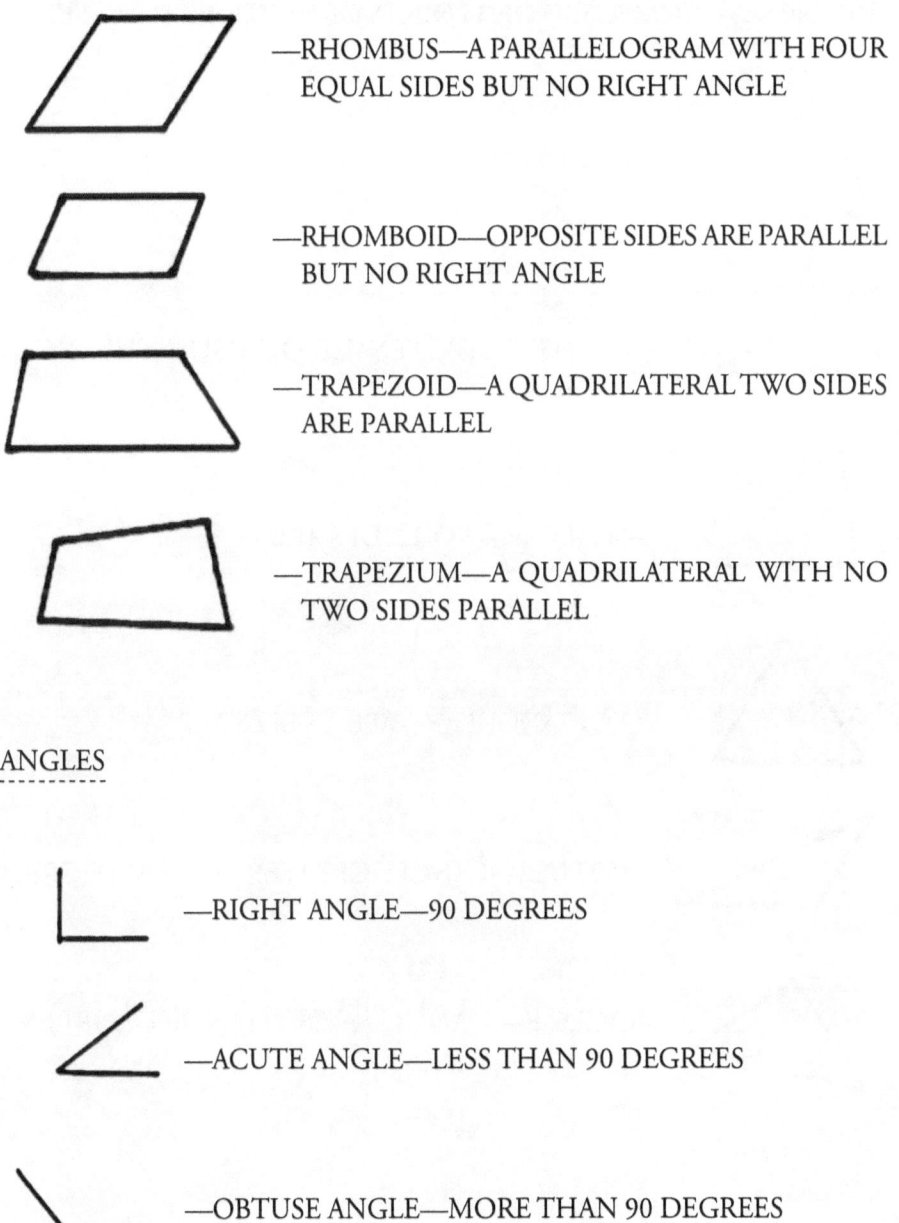

—RHOMBUS—A PARALLELOGRAM WITH FOUR EQUAL SIDES BUT NO RIGHT ANGLE

—RHOMBOID—OPPOSITE SIDES ARE PARALLEL BUT NO RIGHT ANGLE

—TRAPEZOID—A QUADRILATERAL TWO SIDES ARE PARALLEL

—TRAPEZIUM—A QUADRILATERAL WITH NO TWO SIDES PARALLEL

ANGLES

—RIGHT ANGLE—90 DEGREES

—ACUTE ANGLE—LESS THAN 90 DEGREES

—OBTUSE ANGLE—MORE THAN 90 DEGREES

TRIANGLES—COMPOSED OF 3 POINTS OR VERTICES AND 3 SIDES

 —ISOSCELES—2 SIDES =

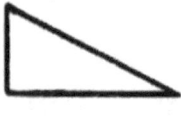 —RIGHT—HYPOTENUSE OPPOSITE THE RIGHT ANGLE

 —SCALENE—NO 2 SIDES ARE =

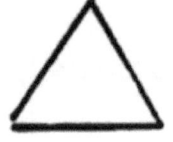 —EQUIANGULAR—ALL ANGLES ARE =

 —OBTUSE—1 ANGLE GREATER THAN 90 DEGREES

 —ACUTE—1 ANGLE LESS THAN 90 DEGREES

FORMULAS

AREA = A X B

PERIMETER = IS THE SUM OF THE BOUNDERY OF A FIGURE

CIRCLE—(AREA = r^2) (CIRCUMFERENCE = 2 X R^2)

TRIANGLE—$A = \dfrac{bh}{2}$

TRAPEZOID—$A = \dfrac{B+b}{2}$ x h (B & b = PARALLEL BASES)

MEASUREMENTS
****

1	INCH	= 2.5 CENTIMETER (APPROX.)
12	INCHES	= 1 FOOT
3	FEET	= 1 YARD

1	CENTIMETER	= 10 MILLIMETER
1	METER	= 100 CENTIMETER = 1.9 YARDS
1	KILOMETER	= 1000 METERS
1	MILE (5280 FT)	= 2.2 KILOMETERS (APPROX.) = 2,200 METERS
6	FEET	= 1 FATHOM

1	KILO	= 2.2 POUNDS (1,000)
1	TON	= 2,000 POUNDS

1	POUND	= 16 OUNCES
1	OUNCE	= 16 DRAMS = 960 MINIMS = 64 C.C.
1	DRAM	= 60 MINIMS OR DROPS = 4 C.C.
1	C.C.	= 15 MINIMS OR DROPS = 1/4 DRAM

1	PINT	= 500 CUBIC CENTIMETERS (C.C.)
2	PINTS	= 1 QUART = 1 LITER (APPROX.) = 1,000 C.C.
4	QUARTS	= 1 GALLON = 4 LITERS = 8 PINTS

1	SCORE	= 20
1	QUIRE	= 24 SHEETS
20	QUIRES	= 1 REAM

1	HECTARES	= 2.47 ACRES

—ANGSTROM UNIT ... $10^{-8\ cm}$ (1/100,000,000 cm)

—MICRON .... 10^{-6} m (1/1,000,000 of a meter)

　　　　or　　　　　　　10^{-3} mm (1/1000 of a millimeter)

—MILLIMICRON .... 10^{-9} m (1/1,000,000,000 of a meter)

—MICROMICRON ...... 10^{-12} m (1/1,000,000,000,000 of meter)

GREATER OR LESSER SIGNS—LESSER NUMBER TO THE POINTED ANGLE ex. 2< is really the same as >2 (less than 2)

10^{9}	–	GIGA	–	G
10^{6}	–	MEGA	–	M
10^{3}	–	KILO	–	K
10^{-1}	–	DECI	–	d
10^{-3}	–	MILLI	–	m
10^{-6}	–	MICRO	–	u
10^{-9}	–	NANO	–	n
10^{-12}	–	PICO	–	p

MEDICINE
****

NUMBER OF BONES
VERTEBRAE 26
SKULL 22
HYOID BONE 1   LONGEST BONE—FEMUR
RIBS & STERNUM 25   SMALLEST BONE—OSSICLE (EAR)
UPPER EXTREMITIES 64
LOWER EXTREMITIES
    INCLUDING PATELLAE ..62
AUDITORY OSSICLES 6
                            _____
                             206

SENSES—SIGHT
        HEARING
        SMELL
        TASTE
        TOUCH   KINESTHETIC—MUSCLE MOVEMENT

BASIC TASTES
        SWEET
        SOUR
        SALT
        BITTER

MICRO-ORGANISMS
        VIRUS
        BACTERIA
        FUNGUS

NEARSIGHTEDNESS (MYOPIA)—CLEAR VISION AT NEAR DISTANCE
FARSIGHTEDNESS (HYPEROPIA) CLEAR VISION AT FAR DISTANCE

NORMAL BLOOD PRESSURE—140/90 mm Hg

VITAMINS

A .... CONDITIONING OF CELLS ESPECIALLY THE RETINA
B 1 .... THIAMINE—CARBOHYDRATE METABOLISM
B 2 .... RIBOFLAVIN—PROTEIN METABOLISM
B 6 .... PYRIDOXINE—NITROGEN METABOLISM
B 12 .... COBALAMINS—NEURAL AND RED BLOOD CELL
                   FUNCTIONS
BIOTIN .... AMINO ACID AND FATTY ACID METABOLISM
C .... ASCORBIC ACID—VASCULAR AND WOUND
                   HEALING FUNCTIONS
D .... BONE GROWTH
E .... CELL AND MEMBRANE GROWTH
FOLIC ACID .. RED BLOOD CELL GROWTH
K .... BLOOD COAGULATION
NIACIN .... NICOTINIC ACID-OXIDATION-REDUCTION
REACTIONS

MINERAL

SODIUM (NA) ..... MUSCLE AND NERVE CONTRACTIONS
POTASSIUM (K) .. MUSCLE AND NERVE RELAXATIONS
CALCIUM (CA) ... BONE AND TOOTH FORMATION AND
                   MUSCLE CONTRACTION
IRON (FE) .... HEMOGLOBIN FORMATION
FLUORINE (FL) ... PREVENTS DENTAL CARIES
IODINE (I) .... THYROID FUNCTIONS

GENETICS
***************D

DNA...DEOXYRIBONUCLEIC ACID RNA...RIBONUCLEIC ACID

CHROMOSOMES

FEMALE—22 PAIRS WITH A PAIR OF XY
MALE—22 PAIRS WITH A PAIR OF XX

MONEY
****

COINS
****

CENT .... ABRAHAM LINCOLN
NICKEL .... THOMAS JEFFERSON
DIME .... FRANKLIN D. ROOSEVELT
QUARTER .... GEORGE WASHINGTON
HALF DOLLAR .... JOHN F. KENNEDY
DOLLAR .... DWIGHT D. EISENHOWER

CURRENCY (BILLS)
****

$1—GEORGE WASHINGTON
 2—THOMAS JEFFERSON
 5—ABRAHAM LINCOLN
 10—ALEXANDER HAMILTON
 20—ANDREW JACKSON
 50—ULYSSES S. GRANT
 100—BENJAMIN FRANKLIN
 500—WILLIAM McKINLEY
 1000—GLOVER CLEVELAND
 5000—JAMES MADISON
 10,000—SOLOMON P. CHASE
 100,000—WOODROW WILSON

MUSIC
****

NOTES

CLASSIC - DO RE MI FA SOL LA TI DO
MODERN - C D E F G A B C

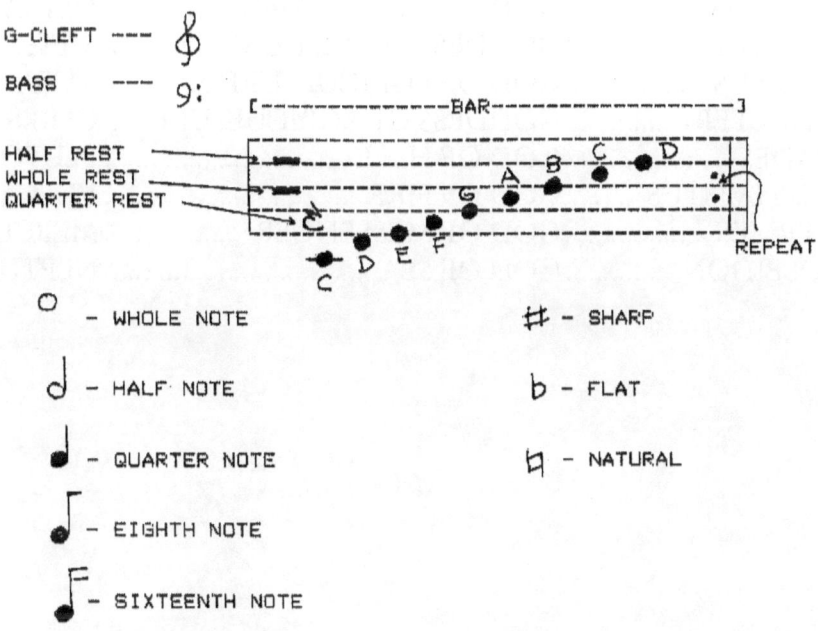

O – WHOLE NOTE

♩ – HALF NOTE

♩ – QUARTER NOTE

♪ – EIGHTH NOTE

♬ – SIXTEENTH NOTE

♯ – SHARP

♭ – FLAT

♮ – NATURAL

MYTHOLOGY
****

GREEK		ROMAN
ZEUS	GOD OF GODS	JUPITER
APHRODITE	GODDESS OF LOVE	VENUS
APOLLO	GOD OF ARTS	
ARES	GOD OF WAR	MARS
ARTEMIS	GODDESS OF WOMEN	DIANA
ATHENA	GODDESS OF WISDOM	MINERVA
CRONUS	GOD OF AGRICULTURE	SATURN
DEMETER	GODDESS OF AGRICULTURE	CERES
HADES	GOD OF HELL	PLUTO
HEPHAESTUS	GOD OF FIRE	VULCAN
HERMES	GOD OF MESSENGER	MERCURY
POSEIDON	GOD OF SEA	NEPTUNE

NUMBERS
****

ROMAN NUMERALS

1 - I	11 - XI	30 - XXX
2 - II	12 - XII	40 - XL
3 - III	13 - XIII	50 - L
4 - IV	14 - XIV	60 - LX
5 - V	15 - XV	90 - XC
6 - VI	16 - XVI	100 - C
7 - VII	17 - XVII	200 - CC
8 - VIII	18 - XVIII	400 - CD
9 - IX	19 - XIX	500 - D
10 - X	20 - XX	900 - CM
		1000 - M

5,000—$\overline{V}$	100,000—$\overline{C}$
10,000—$\overline{X}$	500,000—$\overline{D}$
50,000—$\overline{L}$	1,000,000—$\overline{M}$

NUMBER OF ZEROS

MILLION—6 ....10^6

BILLION—9 ....10^9

TRILLION—12 .... 10^{12}

QUADRILLION—15 ....10^{15}

QUINTILLION—18 .... 10^{18}

PHOBIAS—EXCESSIVE FEARS
****

ALONE .... AUTOPHOBIA
ANIMALS .... ZOOPHOBIA
BEING TOUCHED .... HAPTEPHOBIA
BURIED ALIVE .... TAPHEPHOBIA
CATS .... ALLUROPHOBIA
CLOSED SPACES .... CLAUSTROPHOBIA
CONTAMINATION .... MYSOPHOBIA
CROSSING STREETS .... DROMOPHOBIA
CROWDS .... DEMOPHOBIA
DARKNESS .... NYCTOPHOBIA
DEATH .... THANAPHOBIA
DEPTH .... BATHOPHOBIA
DOGS .... CYNOPHOBIA
EATING FOOD .... SITOPHOBIA
EVERYTHING .... PANPHOBIA
FALLING ASLEEP .... HYPNOPHOBIA
HEART DISEASE .... CARDIOPHOBIA
HEIGHT .... ACROPHOBIA
LANDSCAPE .... XEROPHOBIA
LIGHT .... PHOTOPHOBIA
MEN .... ANDROPHOBIA
MICE .... MUSOPHOBIA
NEW THINGS .... NEOPHOBIA
OPEN SPACES .... AGORAPHOBIA
PAIN .... ALGOPHOBIA
POISON .... TOXICOPHOBIA
SEX .... GENOPHOBIA
SNAKES .... OPHIDIOPHOBIA
STRANGERS .... XENOPHOBIA
THUNDER & LIGHTNING .... ASTRAPHOBIA
WATER .... HYDROPHOBIA
WOMEN .... GYNOPHOBIA

PHYSICS
****

3 KINDS OF MATTER

SOLID
GAS
LIQUID

SPEED—RATE OF MOTION
VELOCITY—SPEED PER DIRECTION

SOUND—1,100 FT/SEC
LIGHT—186,000 MI/SEC = 300,000 KM/SEC

CENTRIFUGAL—FORCE AWAY FROM CENTER
CENTRIPETAL—FORCE TO THE CENTER

ION—A CHARGE PARTICLE
ATOM—SMALLEST UNIT OF A CHEMICAL ELEMENT e.g. NA &
        CL
MOLECULE—SMALLEST PART OF A CHEMICAL SUBSTANCE e.g.
            NACL
ELEMENT—SIMPLEST SUBSTANCE

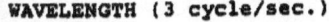

WAVELENGTH (3 cycle/sec.)

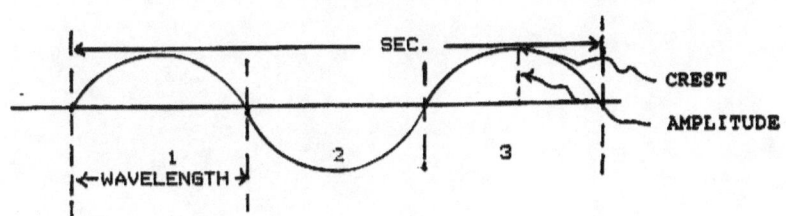

	(Freq) cycles/sec	Wavelength
RADIO WAVES	1.0×10^5	3×10^5 cm
INFRARED	3.0×10^{12}	0.01 cm
VISIBLE LIGHT	4.3×10^{14}	0.00007 cm (7000 A)
ULTRAVIOLET	7.5×10^{14}	4000 A
X-RAY	3.0×10^{18}	$1 A = 10^{-8}$ cm

Frequency—number of vibrations/sec.

PLANETS
****

	SYMBOLS	SIZE (#1 smallest)

DISTANCE FROM SUN .... (☉)

    [
MERCURY ..... (☿) 2

    [
VENUS .... (♀) 4

    [
EARTH .... (♁) 5

    [
MARS .... (♂) 3

    [
JUPITER .... (♃) 9

    [
SATURN .... (♄) 8

    [
URANUS .... (♅) 6

    [
NEPTUNE ..... (♆) 7

    [
PLUTO .... (♇) 1

RANKS
****

MILITARY	AIR	NAVY
PRIVATE	AIRMAN	ENSIGN
CORPORAL	SARGEANT	LT. JUNIOR
SARGEANT	LIEUTENANT	LIEUTENANT
LIEUTENANT	CAPTAIN	LT. COMMANDER
CAPTAIN	MAJOR	COMMANDER
MAJOR	LT. COLONEL	CAPTAIN
COLONEL	COLONEL	COMMODORE
BRIGADIER GENERAL	BRIGADIER GENERAL	REAR ADMIRAL
MAJOR GENERAL	MAJOR GENERAL	VICE ADMIRAL
LIEUTENANT GENERAL	LT. GENERAL	ADMIRAL
GENERAL	GENERAL	FLEET ADMIRAL

BOY SCOUT	GIRL SCOUT	CATHOLIC CHURCH
CUB	BROWNIE	DEACON
DEN	JUNIOR	PRIEST
TENDERFOOT	CADETTE	BISHOP
EAGLE	SENIOR	ARCHBISHOP
		CARDINAL
		POPE

RELIGIONS
****

ATHEISM .... NO GOD
BUDDHISM .... SPIRIT (NO DEFINITE GOD)
CHRISTIANITY .... JESUS CHRIST
EGYPTIAN .... RE AND OSIRIS
GREEK .... HALF GOD AND HALF MAN
HINDUISM .... BRAHMAN
ISLAM .... ALLAH
JUDAISM .... YAHWEH
PREHISTORIC .... TOTEM
TAOISM .... SPIRIT (NO DEFINITE GOD)

APOSTLES OR DISCIPLES OF CHRIST

1. PETER
2. JAMES
3. JOHN
4. ANDREW
5. PHILIP
6. BARTHOLOMEW
7. MATTHEW
8. THOMAS
9. JAMES
10. THADDEUS
11. SIMON
12. JUDAS ISCARIOT

BUDDHA—FOUNDER AND LEADER OF BUDDHISM
CONFUCIUS—FOUNDER AND LEADER OF CONFUCIANISM

RELIGION
****

OUR LORD'S PRAYER

OUR FATHER WHO ART IN HEAVEN
HALLOWED BE THY NAME
THY KINGDOM COME
THY WILL BE DONE ON EARTH AS IT IS IN HEAVEN
GIVE US THIS DAY OUR DAILY BREAD
AND FORGIVE US OUR TREPASSES
AS WE FORGIVE THOSE WHO TREPASS AGAINST US
AND LEAD US NOT INTO TEMPTATION
BUT DELIVER US FROM EVIL

TEN COMMANDMENTS

1. THOU SHALT HAVE NO OTHER GODS BEFORE ME
2. THOU SHALT NOT MAKE UNTO THEE ANY GRAVEN IMAGE
3. THOU SHALT NOT TAKE THE NAME OF THE LORD THY GOD IN VAIN
4. REMEMBER TO KEEP HOLY THE SABBATH DAY
5. HONOR THY FATHER AND THY MOTHER
6. THOU SHALT NOT KILL
7. THOU SHALT NOT COMMIT ADULTERY
8. THOU SHALT NOT STEAL
9. THOU SHALT NOT BEAR FALSE WITNESS AGAINST THY NEIGHBOR
10. THOU SHALT NOT COVET ANYTHING THAT IS THY NEIGHBORS.

SCIENCE
****

TELESCOPE—FOR LONG DISTANT MAGNIFICATION

BINOCULAR—NEAR DISTANT ENLARGEMENT

MICROSCOPE—ENLARGEMENT OF MINUTE PARTICLES OR NOT VISIBLE TO THE NAKED EYE

PERISCOPE—OPTICAL INSTRUMENT WHERE OBJECTS ARE VIEWED BEHIND OBSTACLES OR BARRIER

SCIENCE
****

TEMPERATURE

(CELSIUS)—(FAHRENHEIT)

100 deg.—[ ]—212 deg. (BOILING POINT)
        [ ]
        [ ]
        [ ]
        [ ]
 40 deg.—[ ]—105 deg.
        [ ]
 37 deg.—[ ]—98.6 deg. (NORMAL BODY TEMPERATURE)
        [ ]
  0 deg.—[ ]—32 deg. (FREEZING POINT)
        [ ]
      -- --
     [   ]

CELSIUS OR CENTIGRADE

FORMULA .... $F = C \times 1.8 + 32$

$$C = \frac{F - 32}{1.8}$$

SPELLING
****

ACCOMMODATION
ACCUMULATION
BAZAAR
BELIEVE
BIZARRE
COMMISSION
COMMITMENT
EIGHTH
HORS—D'OEUVRE (OR DURV)
MAYONNAISE
OCCUR—OCCURRED
PAVILION—AUXILIARY
PERSONNEL
PRIVILEGE
RECEIPT
RECIDIVIST
RECEIVE
REFER—REFERRED
RELIEVE
RENAISSANCE
SINCERELY
STRAIGHT
STRENGTH
SUBTLY
TWELFTH
TWENTIETH

PLAN—PLANNING
PLANE—PLANING
SCARE—SCARED
SCAR—SCARRED
MONSIGNOR—MSGR
STAR—STARRING
STARE—STARING

SPORTS
****

TABLE TENNIS (PING-PONG) ..... 9 FT x 5 FT
BOXING RING .... 16-24 FT x 16-24 FT
LAWN TENNIS COURT .... 78 FT x 36 FT
BOWLING LANE .... 76 FT x 3 1/2 FT
VOLLEYBALL COURT .... 60 FT x 30 FT
RACKETBALL COURT................... 60 FT x 30 FT
BASKETBALL COURT.................... 94 FT x 50 FT
BASEBALL INFIELD .... 90 FT x 90 FT
ICE HOCKEY FIELD .... 200 FT x 85 FT
FIELD HOCKEY............................. 100 YDS x 60 YDS
FOOTBALL FIELD .... 100 YDS x 75 YDS

BOXING WEIGHTS

FLYWEIGHT.. 112 LBS
BANTAMWEIGHT................................... 119 LBS
FEATHERWEIGHT .... 125 LBS
LIGHTWEIGHT....................................... 132 LBS
LIGHT-WELTERWEIGHT...................... 139 LBS
WELTERWEIGHT................................... 147 LBS
LIGHT-MIDDLEWEIGHT .... 156 LBS
MIDDLEWEIGHT .... 165 LBS
LIGHT-HEAVYWEIGHT (CRUISER) ... 178 LBS
HEAVYWEIGHT .... 178+LBS

SYMBOLS
****

>............IS GREATER   )

)-LESSER NUMBER NEAR POINTED END

<............IS LESS THAN   )

≠ ....NOT EQUAL

≈ ....SIMILAR TO

≅ ....IS CONGRUENT

∝ ....DIRECTLY PROPORTIONAL

:.............RATIO

∞...........INFINITY

π............Pi

&, ε ....AMPERSAND—AND

*............ASTERISK SEE FOOT NOTE

†............ALSO SEE FOOT NOTE

¶............PARAGRAPH

"............DITTO—SAME

^............CARET—TO BE INSERTED; ABOVE A LETTER A
                    RETROFLEXION SOUND

'............APOSTROPHE—OMISSION OF A LETTER OR MORE

Ñ ....TILDE (TO PRONOUNCE IN SPANISH LIKE (NIE)

© ....COPYRIGHT

® ....REGISTERED COPYRIGHT

♂............MALE

♀............FEMALE

° ............UNDETERMINED SEX

☉ ....SUN—GOLD

☾ ....MOON—SILVER

♁ ....EARTH

☿ ....MERCURY

♃ ....JUPITER

♄ ....SATURN—LEAD

♀...........VENUS

Ag ....SILVER	Pt .... PLATINUM
Au ....GOLD	Pu............ PLUTONIUM
Cu..............COPPER	Ra............ RADIUM
Hg ....MERCURY	Sn............ TIN
K................POTASSIUM	U .... URANIUM
Na..............SODIUM	W .... TUNGSTEN
Pb ....LEAD	
Fe................IRON	

See MEDICINE for more symbols

SEVEN WONDERS OF THE WORLD

****

1) PYRAMID OF EGYPT
2) THE HANGING GARDEN OF BABYLON
3) THE TOMB OF MAUSOLUS
4) THE TEMPLE OF ARTEMIS
5) THE COLOSSUS OF RHODES
6) THE STATUE OF ZEUS
7) THE PHAROS OF ALEXANDRIA

WORDS WITH 1 VOWEL AND 6 OR MORE CONSONANTS

****

CRYPTIC
PHYLLUM
PHYSICS
STRENGTH
STRETCH
STYPTIC
SYMPHONY
SYMPTOM
SYNCHRONY
SYNGAMY
SYNONYMY
TWELFTH
TYRANNY

WORDS-ANAGRAM
****

ARCHES	SEARCH	DISCRETION	DIRECTIONS
BADE	BEAD	FORMER	REFORM
CHUM	MUCH		
DROP	PROD		
EASEL	LEASE		
FLEA	LEAF		
GLEAN	ANGEL		
KNEE	KEEN		
LAME	MALE		
LARGE	LAGER		
LEAD	DEAL		
OPEN	PEON		
REEF	FREE		
SAME	SEAM		
TOUR	ROUT		
TRITE	TITER		

WORDS-ANAGRAM-3 WORDS OR MORE
****

AIDS	— SAID	— DAIS		
ALES	— SALES	— SEAL		
ANEW	— WAVE	— WEAN		
DARE	— READ	— DEAR		
DOER	— RODE	— REDO		
PALMS	— LAMPS	— PSALM		
EMIT	— ITEM	— TIME	— MITE	
EVIL	— LIVE	— VEIL	— VILE	
TEAM	— MATE	— MEAT	— TAME	
TIDE	— EDIT	— TIED	— DIET	
PART	— TRAP	— RAPT	— TARP	— PRAT
PEAL	— PALE	— LEAP	— PLEA	
PEAR	— REAP	— RAPE	— APER	
LARGE	— GLARE	— REGAL	— LAGER	
MANE	— NAME	— MEAN	— AMEN	
SMILE	— SLIME	— LIMES	— MILES	
STEAK	— TEAKS	— SKATE	— TAKES	— STAKE

PATERNAL — PRENATAL — PARENTAL

WORDS-MULTIPLE SIMILAR LETTERS IN A WORD

****

ADDEND
AGGREGATE   HORROR
ASSASSIN   LULL
ASSESS   LULLABY
BANANA   MIRROR
BOBBIN   MONOPOLY
BLEEDER   NEEDLE
BLUBBER   NUNNERY
BUBBLE   PAPAYA
CELLULAR   PEPPER
CANNON   REMEMBER
COMMISSION   SURURRUS (WHISPER)
COMMITMENT   TATTER
COMMITTEE   TATOO
CONCOCT   TRESPASS
CONNECTION   VENEER
FREEZER   VOODOO
GAGGER
GAGGLE
GURGGLE

WORDS WITH NO VOWEL
****

CRY	STY
DRY	STYMY
FRY	STYX
MY	SYLPH
PLY	THY
PRY	TRY
SLY	WRY
SPY	HYMN

WORDS-HOMONYMS (SAME SOUND)-DIFFERENT MEANINGS-SPELLED SAME

****

BOIL
BUST
FAN
LIGHT
RIGHT
RING
ROSE
SHOOT
SPRING
TIE
TIRE
WATCH
WICK

WORDS-PALINDROME-SPELL THE SAME FORWARD AS BACKWARD

****

BOB
BOOB
BIB
CIVIC
DAD
DEIFIED
DID
DUD
EVE
EWE
EYE
GAG
GIG
LEVEL
MADAM
MOM
MUM
NOON
NUN

PEEP
PIP
POOP
POP
RADAR
ROTOR
SHAHS
TAT
TENET
TET—CHINESE NEW YEAR
TIT
TOT
WOW

WORDS-HOMOPHONES—SAME SOUNDS—

DIFFERENT MEANINGS

****

ATE	EIGHT
BARE	BEAR
BEAT	BEET
BORED	BOARD
BREAK	BRAKE
BUY	BY—BYE
CEREAL	SERIAL
CITE	SIGHT
DEAR	DEER
DICE	DIES
EYES	ICE
FAIR	FARE
FOR	FOUR
HAIR	HARE
KEY	QUAY
LICE	LIES
OAT	AUGHT
PAIR	PARE—PEAR
PEAK	PEEK
RICE	RISE
SEA	SEE
TOAD	TOWED
WOOD	WOULD

1 WORD HETERONYM SAME SPELLING WITH 2 PRONUNCIATIONS
                  DIFFERENT MEANINGS

CONDUCT
CONSOLE
CONTEST
CONTRACT
CONVERSE
INVALID
LEAD
LEARNED
LIVE
PRESENT
PUTTING
READ

WORDS-REVERSE
****

ARE	ERA	LOOP	POOL	SPORTS	STROPS
BAN	NAB	LOOT	TOOL	SPOT	TOPS
BRAG	GARB	MAD	DAM	STRAP	PARTS
BIRD	DRIB	MART	TRAM	TAB	BAT
BUT	TUB	MAY	YAM	TANG	GNAT
DIAL	LAID	MUG	GUM	TEEM	MEET
DOG	GOD	NET	TEN	TEN	NET
DECAL	LACED	NEW	WEN	TIDE	EDIT
DEER	REED	NIP	PIN	TOP	POT
DEW	WED	NOT	TON	TORT	TROT
DOOM	MOOD	ON	NO	WAR	RAW
DOT	TOD	PART	TRAP	WARD	DRAW
DRAB	BARD	PAL	LAP	WAS	SAW
DRAWER	REWARD	PAN	NAP	WETS	STEW
EMIT	TIME	PAT	TAP	WOLF	FLOW
GAL	LAG	PIT	TIP	YARD	DRAY
GAS	SAG	POTS	STOP		
GEL	LEG	PRAT	TARP		
GOT	TOG	RIAL	LAIR		
LAGER	REGAL	RAM	MAR		
LEPER	REPEL	RAT	TAR		
LEVER	REVEL	RATS	STAR		
LIVE	EVIL	RECAP	PACER		
LIVED	DEVIL				

ACRONYMS
****

ACTH ...............ADRENOCORTICOTROPIC HORMONE
ASAP ....AS SOON AS POSSIBLE
ASPCA...............AMERICAN SOCIETY FOR PREVENTION OF
                 CRUELTY TO ANIMALS
AWOL ....ABSENCE WITHOUT LEAVE
DVD...................DIGITAL VIDEO DISC
EPA....................ENVIRONMENTAL PROTECTION AGENCY
FDIC..................FEDERAL DEPOSIT INSURANCE CORPORATION
HIV ....HUMAN IMMUNITY DEFICIENCY VIRUS
AIDS..................ACQUIRED IMMUNED DEFICIENCY DISEASE
HMO ....HEALTH MAINTENANCE ORGANIZATION
HIPPA ....HEALTH INFORMATION PERSONAL PRIVACY
                 ACT
HUD ....HOUSING URBAN DEVELOPMENT
LED...................LIGHT EMITTING DIODE
MRI...................MAGNETIC RESONANCE IMAGING
N/A....................NOT APPLICABLE
NAACP ....NATIONAL ASSOCIATION FOR THE
                 ADVANCEMENT OF COLORED PEOPLE
NAFTA...............NORTH AMERICAN FREE TRADE AGREEMENT
NASDAQ ....NATIONAL ASSOCIATION OF SECURITIES
                 DEALERS AUTOMATED QUOTATION
                 SYSTEM
NASCAR............NATIONAL ASSOCIATION FOR STOCK CAR
                 AUTORACING
NASA ....NATIONAL AERONAUTICS AND SPACE
                 ADMINISTRATION
NSA....................NATIONAL SECURITY AGENCY
OSHA.................OCCUPATIONAL SAFETY HEALTH
                 ADMINISTRATION
PET ....POSITRON EMITTING TOMOGRAPHY
PLO ....PALESTINIAN LIBERATION ORGANIZATION
PSA....................PROSTATIC SPECIFIC ANTIGEN
PSAT ....PRELIMINARY SCHOLASTIC APTITUDE TEST
REM ....RAPID EYE MOVEMENT

SCUBA...............SELF CONTAINED UNDERWATER BREATHING
APPARATUS
TNT ...................TRINOTROTOLUENE
VCR....................VIDEO CASSETTE RECORDER
WHO ....WORLD HEALTH ORGANIZATION

END